Summary and Analysis
of

The Five Love Languages

The Secret to Love that Lasts

By

Gary Chapman

Book Nerd

Our Free Gift to You

We would like to thank you for being a fan and for reading this series with two free books on affirmations and procrastination. Download your free ebooks now:

Sincerely,

The Book Nerd Team

TABLE OF CONTENTS

Note to readers:
This is an unofficial summary & analysis of Chapman's The Five Love Languages. This summary is designed to enrich your reading experience. Buy the original book here:
https://www.amazon.com/Love-Languages-Secret-that-Lasts-ebook/dp/B00OICLVBI/

Chapter One Summary of The Five Love Languages

The chapter begins when a friend asks Chapman, the author, why love seems to disappear after marriage. This friend has been married three time. Many people have asked themselves this question or have asked others why love dissipates after marriage. Most people want romantic love in a marriage because popular culture talks about, and it's part of our psychology. Couples seem to have a hard time implementing tips and advice about marriage. All those articles may offer good advice, but a lot of that advice doesn't present the five love languages which people speak. People typically speak their primary language best and the same is true with love. A spouse must learn the primary love language of his or her partner.

Chapman has been a marriage counselor for thirty year, and he discovered that there are five emotional love languages. These languages are the way people show and understand love. There are also numerous love dialects which can often be read about in articles such as "10 ways to show your love." Spouses rarely share the same primary love language. Chapman believes that once couples learn one another's love language, they may have a long lasting marriage.

Chapter Two Summary of The Five Love Languages

Many belief systems, philosophical systems, and secular society agree that love is important and plays a big role in life. The word love is used almost ubiquitously. Children have emotional needs of love and affection that need to be met. If they are not met, a child will grow up with emotional and social challenges. Children misbehave when their love tank is empty. Children begin to seek love in the wrong ways when they don't feel loved. There was a case of a girl named Ashley who was at a psychiatrist's office at age thirteen when she was undergoing treatment for an STD. It turns out that her parents got divorced, and they met her physical need but didn't cater to her emotional needs until it was too late and she got an STD. The parents were confused because they thought they gave her plenty of love, but it turns out that they didn't speak her love language.

People need love for their whole life and need it before they even fall in love. The "in love" phase doesn't last long and the need for loves shows up again because that is part of human nature. Materialism is not a substitute for emotional love.

Couples have a love tank too. Marriage is supposed to allow people to feel loved and be intimate, and solitary confinement is a cruel punishment. Chapman has interviewed couples across the U.S. who talk about their marriage, and their stories are included in this book but their names have been changed. One shouldn't run a marriage on "an empty love tank."

Chapter Three Summary of The Five Love Languages

Chapmen has a friend who came to his office one day and said she was getting married after dating a guy for three weeks. She was thirty-six and had a number of failed relationships but had never been married. People believe that feeling in love is a great foundation to build a marriage on. A lot of couples who are in love assume they'll never become like those couples who argue and break up. The "in-love" experience usually last for about two years according the psychologist Dorothy Tennov. It's likely a good thing that people don't stay obsessed with each other because students in love may fail their classes and others in love may lose their jobs because they become preoccupied with their beloved. People who are in a state of euphoria lose interest in everything except their loved one. People are egocentric by nature and no one is fully altruistic. Once the two year period is up, people start to become more individualistic and less intimate. Some couples think that when they no longer feel in-love they either have to find a new partner or learn to love again without the emotional high. Research shows that second marriages have a sixty percent divorce rate; it's even higher if there are kids involved. People have a need to be truly loved but not to fall in love.

True love starts when euphoric love ends. People feel secure when they feel wanted and cared for by their partner. Love should be intentional.

Chapter Four Summary of The Five Love Languages- Words of Affirmation

Chapman has discovered these five love languages:

- Words of affirmation
- Quality time
- Receiving gifts
- Acts of service
- Physical touch

Couples should learn affirmations to build love. It's important to use words of appreciation and positive comment to compliment a partner. Chapman once had a lady come into his office who was complaining about her husband whom she couldn't get to paint the bedroom. Chapman told her not to mention painting the bedroom again and to tell her husband that she appreciates him next time he takes care of something like paying the bills. At first, this lady was disappointed with Chapman's advice but then she tried it, and it solved the problem. Love isn't about getting someone to do what you want, but speaking affirmations will motivate a spouse to be more receptive to concerns because affirming a spouse comes from a place of gratitude.

Encouraging words and **verbal complements** are two dialects of affirmations. Your spouse may want you to compliment him or her in aspects he/she feels insecure or week in. Chapman provides an example of a husband who encourages his wife to write a book after she quit trying many years ago. She was eventually able to get a book contract. If you have a spouse who has great potential, go ahead and encourage him or her to take the next steps. We all have a calling and potential to reach in life so it's important to be surrounded by supportive people who encourage us. Only encourage your partner to pursue what he or she wants, not what you want for him or her. Otherwise, your partner may feel like you're criticizing him or complaining which leads to feelings of rejection. Empathy will allow you to view life from your spouse's perspective and realize what's important to him or her. If your love language isn't positive affirmation, you may struggle to learn this language at first but will get better at it in time.

Also, the tone through which you express feelings is important. For example, saying "I will do the laundry" in a loud or harsh tone will sound judgmental. By stating the same phrase with kindness, you will get a kinder reaction. Love is forgiving and doesn't track wrongs. Forgiveness is a choice and a commitment, not a feeling.

Love doesn't demand anything, but it can request things. Marriages are supposed to be equal partnerships. Each partner needs to know their partner's wants in a successful marriage. It's important for requests not to sound like demands. For example, "it would be nice if we can go visit that town again" is an example of a request. Partners have a choice to respond to requests since love is a choice. You can't force someone to love you. Don't shame or guilt a spouse into doing something for you because that's not love.

Humans have a deep desire to feel appreciated, and that's why affirmations are important. You can write down affirmations that inspire you if they are not your primary love language. Inspiration for affirmative words can be found on social media, book, or even movies. You can say something nice about your spouse to a family member, or say something nice about your spouse in front of others. Chapman met a couple who disagreed about almost everything so he told them separately to write down the things they liked about one another and say positive affirmations for two months. That exercise improved the marriage significantly.

Chapter Five Summary of The Five Love Languages- Quality Time

Quality time means giving someone all of your attention. Of the couple in the previous chapter, the wife wasn't that happy with affirmative words because it wasn't her primary love language. The affirmation made marriage a little better for the wife, but they made the husband very happy. The wife's primary love language is quality time. Chapman called the husband to let him know that his wife's love language is quality time. The husband agreed with him and said he used to spend a lot of time with his wife before they got married. Chapman told the husband to list the things his wife enjoys. Quality time spent means time without the phone, the TV, and without other distraction. It could meant taking a trip as a couple or going to a café or simply talking to each other about one's day. Chapman instructs the husband to spend quality time with his spouse once a week even though he has a demanding corporate job. The husband makes time for his wife, and many years later the couple is still in a happy marriage. The husband has even started his own company and is doing well. Both of their love tanks remain full.

It's important to spend time together without distractions and give your spouse your undivided attention. Two people or even a family can live in the same house but live completely different lives as if they're not together. It's important for couples to focus on one another when they spend time together. Spending time together isn't about doing the activity together, it's about the feeling that activity creates. The same applies to parents who spend time with their kids; it's about the bonding and positive feelings that parents create with their kids when they play a game together.

Quality conversation is one dialect of **quality time**. Couples should share their sympathetic feelings and wishes with each other. When someone says their spouse doesn't talk, they really mean their spouse doesn't talk about sympathetic things. Affirmative words are focused on speaking while a quality conversation is focused on listening so they are not the same. Chapman had a client who was upset that he kept giving advice to his wife about her work situation, and she eventually left him. Relationships aren't projects or problems and require attentive listening. Advice should only be given if requested and without sounding like an order. Some general good practices for listening include maintaining eye contact, giving your partner your full attention, confirming the feeling you think your spouse is experiencing, and paying attention to body language. Also, don't interrupt your partner when he or she is speaking. A wife who wants to know how her husband thinks or feels is really looking for intimacy; otherwise, it may be hard for her to connect to him. A lot of grown-ups struggle with revealing their thoughts or feelings because they grew up in households where showing emotion or desires was considered inappropriate. So they learned to keep their feeling to themselves and by the time they grow up, they were out of touch with their emotional side. When a husband says things like "he did the wrong thing" when the wife asks for an opinion, the husband should learn to express his feelings instead of just replying logically. Chapman recommends carrying a notepad and writing down how you feel throughout the day if you want to learn quality conversation. Talk to your spouse about the emotions you felt throughout the day and soon you will get better at expressing feelings. Emotions lead to thoughts which lead to actions; that's why it's important to be in touch with your emotions.

Chapman describes two personality types which he calls "dead seas" and "babbling brooks." The Dead Sea type may experience many things but is happy to keep them to oneself. The babbling brook type expresses whatever he or she sees or hears. The two types tend to attract each other because one is good at listening and the other is good at talking. At some point in a marriage, the babbling brook may feel like he or she knows nothing about his Dead Sea spouse. Conversely, the Dead Sea knows too much about his or her babbling brook spouse and wants some space. The Dead Sea will need to learn to express oneself and the babbling brook will have to get better at listening if things are to work out. Chapman tells both of these types to speak about three things which happen to them each day for a few weeks at minimum.

Another dialect of quality time is quality activities. These are activities which one partner is willing to do while the other one really want to do. Doing these activities is a way to express love for one another and share quality time. It's important to make time for quality activities if this is your partner's primary love language, otherwise the marriage will suffer.

Chapter Six Summary of The Five Love Languages- Receiving Gifts

Chapman says that he has studied anthropology in Chicago. He has studied many cultures and came to realize that giving gifts was a part of courting and marriage as can be seen in many cultures. Hosts give gifts to their guests, and kids give gifts to their parents. Gift giving is part of our culture. Symbols convey emotions. There are couples who always wear their wedding rings and those who never do; this is because people have different attitudes toward the symbolic meaning of a ring. For individuals whose primary love language is gift giving, they will likely value the ring and all the other gift they get. It's not the cost of the gift that matters but the emotion it stirs up in a partner. Gift giving won't come naturally to everyone, and this is one language that may need to be learned. Make a list of the type of gifts your spouse has enjoyed in the past or get someone to help you. If your spouse rejected your gifts in the past, then chance are that it's not his or her primary love language.

Some people enjoy spending money while other like to save or invest it. For the spender, gift giving will be a lot easier. For those who like to save, they may experience resistance when it comes to purchasing a gift for their significant other. However, savers may fail to recognize that by saving and investing they are actually taking care of their own emotional needs. One's significant other might have different emotional needs which involve receiving gifts. The way people treat money reflects their emotional needs. One can think of gift giving as investing in a marriage and filling up a spouse's love tank. Savers will remain savers, but investing in one's marriage is like buying the best stock.

There's something called **the gift of self** which is the need for presence. It's important to be there for a spouse when he or she feels like you are needed. One woman believed that her husband loved softball more than he loved her because he left to play softball after their baby was born and after a funeral. One should be there for a spouse in a moment of crisis because one's presence becomes the symbol of love; presence is the gift in this situation, and a spouse whose primary love language is gift giving needs her or his partner to be present. If your primary language is gift giving, you need to tell that to your partner if you want him or her to be present. One shouldn't expect a spouse to read one's mind. Giving appears to be the basis of love. Gifts can also be handmade or they can be a live plants.

Don't reject your partner's feelings or make fun of them. Don't assume your partner "should" be happy because he or she appears to have it all; really listen to your partner or they will feel rejected. Try giving your partner gifts for one week if your partner's primary love language is gifts.

Summary and Analysis of The Five Love Languages

Chapter Seven Summary of The Five Love Languages- Acts of Service

Some examples of acts of service can include washing the car, taking care of bills, taking kids to school, cooking dinner, paying the bills, or reorganizing the closet. These things should be done with a positive attitude.

There was a young couple who Chapman spoke with, and they disagreed on everything according to the husband. Chapman had them list four acts of service that they would like to see their partner doing. Both husband and wife have acts of service as their primary love language in this anecdote, but their dialect is different. These acts of service are expressions of love and aren't mandatory. Love doesn't demand anything and is given freely, but partners can make requests to point love in the right direction. A lot of couples behave differently after they get married than the way they acted while they were dating; this is because the euphoria or newness of love wears of and people are influenced by how they grew up and their beliefs about love. It's important to not be critical and demanding because this doesn't come off as loving. However, if you pay attention to the demands of your spouse, you may discover his or her love language.

No person should ever feel like a doormat in a relationship because it's treasonous. Manipulating a partner through guilt and fear is not an act of love. Everyone has their own desires and feelings. Some people will need to drop stereotypes of how a wife or husband should act. Someone who grew up in a traditional home in which the mother cooked and cleaned may need to reexamine that way of living in their own marriage. If a wife's primary love language is acts of service, she will likely need her husband to help with housework to keep her love tank full. Maintaining a stereotype is not rewarding if it puts strain on a marriage or fails to address the emotional needs of a spouse. It's a good idea to keep a list of your partner's requests and ask what his or her top priorities are which would make him or her feel loved if done. You can hire help to do an act of service.

Chapter Eight Summary of The Five Love Languages- Physical Touch

Studies have shown that babies who are interacted with are healthier emotionally. Some babies may develop a condition called failure to thrive at the early stages of their life if they are not held or picked up often by caregivers.

There are many ways to express affection to a spouse through physical touch, and some people's primary love language is physical touch. Nerve cells in the body are not distributed evenly and some skin on the body is more sensitive than other skin. The finger tips and nose tend to be more sensitive. To a child whose love language is physical touch, getting bullied by classmates or spanked by parents is even more hurtful for this type of child because physical touch is a louder messenger. If a child whose primary love language is physical touch gets hugged, this communicates love more strongly to this child than to one whose primary love language is something else.

Ask your spouse how she or he wants to be touched and let them teach you what they like. Don't touch your spouse if he or she finds your touch irritating. Just because you enjoy touching your spouse a certain way, doesn't mean that your spouse enjoys it. Sometimes touching will require your full attention, and at times it may about placing a hand on the shoulder. Learn what your spouse enjoys and study that topic. For example, if your spouse prefers messages, it will behoove you to read some book or watch videos on how to be a good masseur. If you weren't raised in a family which frequently hugs or kisses, there may be a few learning curves for you when it comes to learning this love language. You can try touching in different places and in different ways. For example, giving a kiss once you and your partner get in the car is one thing your partner may enjoy.

Each society has its own customs when it comes to meeting and greeting people as well as treating women appropriately. Couples get to decide what is appropriate for the two of them and how they want to be treated by each other. Open marriages often do not satisfy couples' emotional needs because they break intimacy. For someone whose primary love language is physical touch, infidelity is even more painful.

In times of crisis people often want to be held or hugged. People can't always change their circumstances, but if they are surrounded by loving individuals, it will make it easier to get through a difficult situation. For a spouse whose primary love language is physical touch, this spouse will especially need to be held in a time of crisis. A spouse might never forget the lack of support during a time or crisis. One couple whose house Chapman once stayed at said they discovered each other's love language many years ago and their marriage changed for the better. Physical touch may include holding hands, letting the feet touch when seated, or placing a hand around the spouse when other people are present.

Chapter Nine Summary of The Five Love Languages- What is your primary love language?

It's a good idea to figure out you own primary love language. One person Chapman spoke with didn't hear words of affirmation from his parents often so words of affirmation became one of his love languages. For guys, sexual desire has a physical basis and provides a release. For ladies, physical desire is based on emotions and on whether they feel appreciated and loved. Guys often make the mistake of thinking that physical touch is their primary love language, but this may not be the case. When a couple meet each other's emotional needs and learn to speak each other's primary love language, the sexual issues of their relationship often get worked out by themselves. What your spouse asks you to do often holds clues to his or her primary love language. How you express love to your partner often reflects how you would want to be treated.

Here are three ways to find your primary love language:

1. What do you get hurt by the most that you wish your spouse would do?

2. What to you often request of your partner? These are usually things that would help you feel cared for and loved.

3. How do you show love for your spouse?

The people who have a hard time identifying their primary love language usually have had their love tank full for a long time or empty for a long time, so they're out of touch with what makes them feel loved. Think about what your ideal spouse would act like or what made you fall in love with your spouse in the first place, and you may figure out your primary love language.

Chapman suggests that couples play the Tank Check game. One must ask about the love tank level of one's spouse on a scale from one to ten. Then one should ask how they can fill that love tank. Ask that question three times a week. Once the spouse reaches level ten, then their love tank is full, but one shouldn't quit loving them.

Chapter Ten Summary of The Five Love Languages- Love is by Choice

Expressing love won't change the past, but it makes for a brighter future. Thousands of couples say that are no longer in love with their current partner and want to walk away. Their unfulfilled emotional needs makes them want to look for a new love. The in-love experience usually lasts for up to two years, and after that love is a choice. A person can choose to keep their partner's love tank full. A spouse will continue to feel loved if his or her love tank will keeps getting filled. People rarely fall in love or out of love at the same time. The example provided in this chapter described a guy who didn't love his wife anymore and was in love with another woman. That woman ended up falling out of love with him, and he felt broken. He eventually decided to seek marriage counseling and ended up fixing his marriage three years later. Both he and his wife were very happy. Love isn't always comfortable or comes naturally to us but it serves our partner. It's something we do for them. We have a choice each day.

Chapter Eleven Summary of The Five Love Languages- The Difference Love Makes

People have a need to feel secure, worthy, and significant. Love is often associated with security or self-worth for many people. People often feel significant when they are loved. True love created liberation because people no longer have to focus on their own needs as much and can focus on bigger things. When there is no love in a marriage, couples often fight just to prove self-worth or significance. Difference start to feel like a big deal. People don't feel secure when they don't feel loved.

There was a couple who acted more like roommates. They didn't speak each other's primary love language nor did they know what it was until they spoke to Chapman. About two months after speaking with Chapman, they went off on their second honeymoon.

Chapter Twelve Summary of The Five Love Languages- On loving an Unlovable

Chapman recognized the young woman who was getting marriage counseling when he went for a stroll in the garden with his wife. The young lady asked him if it was possible to love someone she hated. Chapman said he would discuss this question during her next appointment. Chapman knows that when one is angry for a long time, the anger turns into hate. He also knew that he struggled in his marriage during its early years. The young lady's husband wasn't open to marriage counseling or to changing his ways. Chapman asked the young lady to lean on her faith while taking part in an experiment which might save her marriage. He read to her the passage from Luke which encourages all to love one's enemies and bless those who curse one. Chapman wondered if it was possible to love a spouse who one has grown to hate as in the case of the young lady. He wasn't sure if the young lady's husband would ever become loving toward the young lady, but he wanted her to try his experiment. Chapman wanted her to fill her husband's love tank to see if his attitude toward her would change. The young lady was very religious and didn't want to leave her marriage for moral and religious reasons. Chapman told her that staying or leaving the marriage are both painful options. Chapman figured out the love language of the husband by asking the young lady some questions. The young lady said that her love tank has been empty for many years, and after the emotional high wore off her marriage became less loving. The young lady said that she would like to respect and love her husband again. She also wanted to spend more quality time with him and talk to him. She felt like her husband was putting business and other things ahead of her. Chapman said that he wanted the young lady to speak her husband's primary love language for six months and fill up his love tank. If the husband acts more loving toward his wife in six months, than the experiment is a success. We can't force anyone to love us, but acting with kindness and generosity will bring kindness into our lives. Chapman tells the young lady to tell her husband that she wants to be a better wife and to ask the husband if he has any suggestions for her. Chapman tells her to accept the husband's response no matter if it's positive or negative. Chapman also identified the husband's second love language. Chapman tells her to be more physical with her husband and to take initiative since physical touch is one love language of her husband. The young lady said that this will be difficult for her because she's not sexually responsive when her husband ignores her all day. Chapman said it's natural for women to only be responsive when they feel loved, so this was going to be difficult. Women feel used when someone request sexual intimacy without making them feel loved. The young lady said that she would feel like a hypocrite for expressing love to a husband she doesn't love. **Chapman said**

that feeling love and expressing love are two different things. If one is claiming to feel love when one doesn't, this can be viewed as hypocritical by some. The act of love is a choice and is acted upon for the benefit of a partner; this is not hypocritical. Chapman tells the young lady to ask her husband for feedback once a month to see how she's doing and to accept whatever answer he gives. Once he starts to respond positively, Chapman wants the young lady to request something of her husband a week later; it should be something specific that speaks to her love language. For example, she can ask him to take a walk in the garden with her. If the husband starts to say yes to her requests, the young lady will start to have more positive feelings toward her husband. Chapman tells the young lady to write down any complaints in a notebook. He tells her that he will teach her to show frustration and irritation toward her husband in a constructive way.

The experiment worked! The young lady saw a huge shift in her husband's attitude, and she began to regain her loving feelings for him. After four months, the husband responded well to his wife's requests. The husband claims that Chapman is a miracle worker, and he encouraged his wife to keep getting counseling which she did for three more months after the six months. Chapman encourages readers to try this experiment if they are struggling in their marriage. A lot of people saved their marriage by doing this experiment. It's important for couples to stay consistent in their action and keep speaking each other's love language.

Chapter Thirteen Summary of The Five Love Languages- A Note From The Author

You won't know if speaking your spouse's primary love language will improve the marriage until you try to speak it consistently. Chapman says that when the emotional love need is met for a couple, it makes the rest of the marriage more workable. Things just flow better. People often come into marriage with a history, but couples need to find a healthy way to talk about their differences so those differences don't destroy the marriage. Everyone has different perspectives and expectations, but these different ways and viewpoints need to be processed in a healthy marriage. When couples don't feel love, they become withdrawn. It's hard to love someone from whom we don't receive love and this may test one's spirit. Chapman struggled in his own marriage at one point and had to go back to his spiritual roots. He found that God gives the energy of love within one even if love in unrequited. Chapman wrote this book for married couples and for those in the euphoria stage of love. Chapman wants married couples to unleash their full potential for the benefit of all mankind. Chapman wants all children to feel loved so they're not seeking love out there and wasting their energy instead of growing and learning. Chapman appreciates you passing this book on to other people if you feel like it changed your life. You can visit his website at www.fivelovelanguages.com to discuss what you've learned.

Frequently Asked Questions of The Five Love Languages

1. How should one find their primary love language?

One should take a look at how one shows love to other people or what one complains about the most. One should ask one's partner about what one complains about the most. What one requests from one's partner often holds clues to the primary love language. One might discover one's love language through the process of elimination.

2. How can one discover the love language of one's spouse?

Have the spouse read *The Five Love Languages Men's Edition*. Think about what your spouse complains about most often or requests most often. Listening to your spouse's complaints may seem annoying, but these complaints reveal his or her love language.

3. Does one's love language change with age?

Chapman believes that one's love language remain with us for life. Some love languages may speak more strongly to us at different points in our life or during difficult life situations.

4. How do the five love languages apply to children?

Children whose tank isn't full may seek out love in the wrong places when they become teenagers. Children need to learn to receive and give love in all five languages according to Chapman. Children need to receive love, especially in their primary language.

5. Does a child's love language change as he or she gets older?

A child's dialect may change or sometimes parents need to show their love in a more age-appropriate way. Sometimes a teenager may think that the way his or her parents show love is childish.

6. What happens if a spouse's primary love language is difficult to learn?

Practice taking small steps toward learning the language. Use small gestures or spend a little bit of time at first. Make a list of positive statements about your spouse, give your spouse a pat on the back, spend twenty minutes talking one-on-one, or bring your spouse a small gift.

7. Are the love languages gender-slanted?

Chapman hasn't done the research on that and prefers to keep these gender neutral.

8. How did Chapman discover the five love languages?

He realized that people need to be loved in different ways. Chapman studied his notes from twelve years of counseling and found a pattern. This book has sold more than five million English copies and has been translated into more than thirty-eight languages.

9. Do the five love languages apply to all cultures?

A lot of publishers accepted the book and said these principles apply to their country as well; that's why Chapman believes these love languages are universal.

10. Why have the five love languages succeeded?

When people feel loved by their spouse, their outlook on life is usually brighter. Speaking their spouse's love language allows love to be reborn and helps couples once the emotional high of a new relationship begins to subside and differences emerge. The book sells more and more copies each year, and this is likely because couples recommend the book to their friends.

11. What if a spouse doesn't respond to his or her own love language?

It's likely that one is speaking the wrong love language if one's spouse is unresponsive. A spouse may already be involved in another romantic relationship; that's why he or she is not responding. A spouse may perceive the speaking of his love language as manipulation if things have been hostile for a long time. The best thing to do is to continue to speak the love language of your spouse even if they don't treat you well because if you keep going they won't think you're just doing this to manipulate them. If you keep loving your spouse no matter what, this is a way to demonstrate unconditional love.

12. Can a marriage be revived after sexual infidelity?

Chapman has seen many couples heal after sexual infidelity. To fix such a broken relationship, the affair should be broken off and the couple needs to find out what led to the affair in the first place. The spouse who had an affair must change his/her attitude and behavior and examine his personality and beliefs. Couples who experience an affair must look at the patterns in their marriage and be willing to change harmful patterns. Couples will likely need professional counseling- individual and marriage counseling.

13. What should one do when one's spouse doesn't want to speak the love language of their partner?

Love is a choice and can't be demanded. A spouse may be uncomfortable to speak a new love language because he or she may not have grown up in an environment that supported this type of love language. The other reason a spouse might not speak the love language of his or her partner is because he or she fears that her partner will become complacent; this is untrue. Words of love encourage, and that's why it's important to say words of affirmation to kids. Ask your spouse about how full his or her love tank is and ask him or her about how you can fill it.

14. Can love be rekindled in a marriage after it's been gone for three decades?

It can as long as the couple is willing to work on their marriage. One couple was able to bring the love back to their marriage after it was gone for more than two decades.

15. How do the five love languages help singles? A lot of singles have said that this book has helped them in all of their relationships so Chapman decided to write a singles version of this book. One incarcerated young man said that he finally understood that his mother loved him; she just speaks a different love language than he does.

You can take a love languages quiz and find resources at www.fivelovelanguages.com

Analysis and Thoughts on The Five Love Languages

Just as it's important to affirm a spouse, I think it's also important to affirm a friend or even a co-worker when appropriate. If your friend's primary love language is affirmations, than he or she will appreciate hearing your kind words and your friendship will be strengthened. A friend will appreciate a genuine compliment even if this is not your friend's primary love language. It would be great to have a boss who encourages his employees to reach their full potential, but that's not the reality for most people. That's why it's important to have faith in oneself and be one's own cheerleader at times. True leaders must learn to encourage and motivate their team.

It's also important to speak words of encouragement to kids because this will motivate them to do the right thing keep them working toward their goals. Affirming someone is not praising mediocrity; it's actually the fuel which allows one to move forward and feel motivated in life. Parents should practice empathy and not view life only from their own perspective. If a kid wants to join a club or join a team, a parent should encourage the potential in their child instead of forcing a child to join an activity because the parent believes it's beneficial. Parents should have their own life too and reach their own potential instead of living through their kids. Each parent and child has a unique potential and purpose just as couples may have common goals but unique callings in life.

Friends crave quality time as well, especially if this is their primary love language. A friend may feel hurt or grow resentful if his/her best friend never spends time with him or her. Kids also require quality time with their parents, and with their friends too at times. It's important for friends to agree on how they will spend time together. If one friend constantly invites another to places that this friend dislikes, the invited friend may feel like he or she is just dragged along for the ride. This is why it's important to spend quality time doing quality activities. Both parties should have a say in how to spend time because each relationship is a partnership and no one should force another to attend an event that isn't enjoyed by both parties. However, if an activity is very significant to a friend, it is best that one consider attending it so as not to hurt the friend's feelings, and this is where compromising may be beneficial for the friendship. Love means doing something for someone you care about, so spending time in the way your loved one wants shows selflessness and care. Quality conversations are also important to friends whose primary love language is quality time. If a partner or friend is always emotionally distant and never talks about how he or she feels, this will create friction or alienation. At some point, the partner requesting a quality conversation will just get tired of trying to break the walls of his or her partner. The partner who doesn't express feeling may get blindsided when his or her partner leaves or starts to distance oneself. Just as it's important for friends to talk about feelings, it's also important for kids and employees to express their feelings. Kids need to feel understood and loved by their parents, and parents need to be receptive to their kids' emotions and accept them for what they are. Parents who shame their kids for expressing feeling or denying how they feel may end up with emotionally unstable kids; the lack of affirmation may be emotionally abusive. Employees who never have quality conversations with their bosses or co-workers may feel distant from the team and its goals; they may feel unappreciated or marginalized. Making an employee feel appreciated will create a positive work environment and better results, and that's why it's important for leaders to know what motivates their employees.

A co-worker who enjoys working in a team may feel alienated and unproductive when the team never meets to work on a project. Some people thrive when they work in a group environment rather than by themselves.

People shouldn't assume things about their loved ones; instead, one should get to know them and meet their emotional needs while meeting one's own needs. Speaking the love language of a loved one consistently will keep a relationship strong.

Thank you for reading!

We hope you learned something interesting from this summary.

We care about your reading experience here at Book Nerd and want to provide you with thorough and insightful book guides.

We'd like to give you a virtual high five for reading until the very end. You're a great reader!

Before we part ways, do you mind leaving us a review on Amazon? We would appreciate that greatly, and your support will help us create more book guides in the future.

Thanks again! Here is where you can post your review:

Yours Truly,

Book Nerd Team

Don't forget your gift!

https://www.subscribepage.com/2freemindsetebooks

ABOUT BOOK NERD

Book Nerd is dedicated to providing readers with thorough and thoughtful summaries.

38024520R00031

Made in the USA
Middletown, DE
04 March 2019